Natural Chemistry

Natural Chemistry
Michelene Wandor

PUBLICATIONS
2013

Published by Arc Publications
Nanholme Mill, Shaw Wood Road,
Todmorden OL14 6DA, UK
www.arcpublications.co.uk

Copyright © Michelene Wandor 2012
Design by Tony Ward
Printed in Great Britain by the
MPG Book Group, Bodmin and King's Lynn

978 1904614 53 1 pbk
978 1904614 54 8 hbk

ACKNOWLEDGEMENTS
'Samson after Milton' has been set to music
by a student composer; 'Illuminatus' was
performed by Michelene Wandor's early music
group, Siena Ensemble, at the Jewish Museum,
London. 'Ophelia' first appeared in 'Fluviatile', a
collaboration with artist Lindsey Adams.

Cover photograph:
'IgniFolia 12' © Adam Victor, 2013
by kind poermission of the photographer.

Editor for the UK and Ireland:
John W. Clarke

for Adam, Patrizia & Thomas
for Ivan, Sophie, Lila & Oliver

Contents

natural chemistry
for Thomas

Citta della Pieve: a chill hilltop
hands touch closed blooms, holding bright red pistils
at dawn in the chill
> *my love*

hands pick silk saffron crocus petals, long
lines in a semi-arid land; dawn
> dawn

pickers, clean, moist hands stained purple, yellow
crocus sativus, a chill dawn hilltop
in winter
> *my love is*

each corm, below its later proud purple
has stored starch underground for a season
packed in warm earth, away from light, showing
above a striated fragile purple
> *my love is a poem*

the Lord visited Citta, and tasted
crisp saffron flavoured macaroons, lightly
lemon-oranged
the Lord gave Perugino an intense
yellow, to oil the sun with brightness
> *my poem loves and skips*

even though he (Perugino) did not
believe in the immortality of
the soul, just in that of his paintings
> *my love is a boy*

my boy wears purple, a crocus boy, silk cheek nuzzling
> into my neck, soft and sweet

my love skips

painters came to see Perugino's saffron
we come, seeking *zafferano,* my boy
nuzzling, wearing purple among the gold-

red, led round the round church market, wilted
purple in wicker baskets
                              his hands stretch

crocus sativus, unknown in the wild
my boy, his own aphrodisiac now
only sometimes wild
                              like flowers in wicker
baskets

my boy flowers through day and night, a spice
a medicine, my aphrodisiac

my love has skipped a generation

no stigma in loving him, the prized part
deep, dry red fronds in tiny jars, he still
tiny by anyone's gathering

his colour is dry, *his tempera* rich
golden yellow, no common autumn crocus, he
but here for all seasons, blossoming
at dawn, wilted by evening, by his
own light

my love, my boy, his own generation

Goneril

a gecko slips between cracked columns, like
a salamander on the ceiling, no
fool he, smells smoke, no fire, just flaring rage
loving a father will come to nothing

I lied, I knew I lied, and lied again
salt sweat runs down from armpits to waist to
the hollow in the middle of the fire
a fire princess kissing the ice prince cold

France: a man who wooed me with snails and frogs'
legs and garlic and butter, parsley and
fenugreek. He struck a flint with no spark,
no more sweet and viscous onion soup, dark,
with burned edges tasting memories
round, sliced baguettes, charred at the crust's hard edge,
julienne cheese, dry at languid centres
oily where their lean sides meet the air
a darker purpose wreathed, a flare first borne

an idle old man, who forces me, his
eldest daughter, to hate him, him whom I
love as no other
                  late eclipses in the sun and moon, lay
myself to the charge of a star. Daughter
against father, father against his child
no planetary influence can dry
my tears, my villainous melancholy

now I have no prince; take me or leave me
how much like a crab is an apple, a
child, falling from a high tree

apple boy
for Thomas

now, at four months, a champion nuzzler
of shoulders, fist-chewer, dribbler without
a football   *pullke* thighs   and a little
sumo quiff at the back of his neck, at
the nape of his neck

                       just where his mum will
kiss him often and often and always
in the present tense

                  which is always now

now, he curls and flips onto his front, one
arm caught under   face dipping and dipping
till the arm waves free into cocooning time
his bum in the air   his legs dimple-bent
his arms coming after, not tumbling like
tumbling jill in the rhyme above his bed

now not just an apple boy
but an apple turnover boy

is Joan Baez Virginia Woolf's real daughter?

a button bow upper lip, stretching up, to
ward the arch of a proud nose

hair, a winged familiar, swooping
away from mid-forehead
too soon for a widow's peak

in this film, seen for the first time, she
moves Bobby's chair, to make
room for his guitar   she
tilts the neck (of his guitar), so
he can twist the pegs more easily

that's how life is tuned

when they stand, he, full on
the microphone, his harmonica
poised to sound mouth kisses in the middle eight

she, become half-on, poises
on the side, politely leaning
in, her voice licking his
soaring above for a tribute moment
but serving
always serving

kindness, you can't accuse me of

one poetry reading, two halves, two poets
we bring our books; she arranges hers in the middle
                        of the table
oh, my god, she simpers, I hate this photo, it makes me
look just like a poet

she begins, taking more time to talk in
her life's anecdotes than read her poems,
looks at her watch when her allotted time is up, simpers
                        again, tells
more anecdotes, reads a couple of poems

audience polite, thirsty, shuffles cold feet in the under-
                        heated room

I hurry my set, no lifetales, no packdrills; poems
high moral ground, me, I think (*I said you could not accuse*
                        me of kindness)
not a second over my allotted time
I make the audience laugh

she returns, to top the bill
don't try and use me as a curtain-raiser, I think

I told you you could not accuse me of kindness

haiku for Rosie

you ordered your life

and then left early, before

it had all arrived

photography
for Eve Arnold, 1913-2012

camera watches, over her shoulder brushes
light, watches water flash behind her hair
shooting rapids, now so rapidly shooting
speeding faster than just under a hundred
years per second ago

a silent shutter shuts out sounds
making water into metal
in the alchemy of an eye

catching a moment that never was
and never again will
be

like catching at a star which doesn't look like a star
because it is only in the water

on looking for a new bathroom suite
(we hear sweet charity)

a coupling song: to be read
only after the watershed

close coupling of an unusual
kind, kithier than the old style, where
independence and a snake-
like link made the relationship flow
smoothly with never a
flush of embarrassment

close coupling is the new thing
everywhere you look
you can't see
the join between the
            hidden sleek separateness

some would say a rev
olutionary design
smash the old cistern (*we hear*)
and bring in the new
a relative, non-revelatory improvement

listen to this: not a brother
but a cister(n) (*we hear*)
not a flash in the pan
but a new (*we hear noo*)
loo

Esther's book (or atheism)

almost everything in this story may never have happened

of all sacred books, Esther's is the only one that never
                                                    mentions God

Esther *hamalka*, sweet fragrance, spreading goodness
a morning star when other stars have gone

Jews bathe in warm water in the winter, in the summer in cold
The Jews dance
                    the Jews sing
                                    they are happy
they must die, says Haman
                            he hates the Jews

Esther is a dove
                    entering a nest
where a snake lies coiled
                            Esther is like the
planet Venus, which in Greek, is Astara
sweet fragrance, spreading goodness, the dove who
enters the nest where a snake lies coiled

This is the story of a woman and the secret she kept and the
                        secret she told to save her people.

which of us wears the mask?
who holds the earth in their arms?
who made the waters of the sea salt?
the waves with the briny aroma of wine?
who chains the sea so that it shall not overflow the land?

this is the story of Esther
some say the story of Esther is the story of the virtue of
women
perhaps even a fairy tale with the gallows as a moral

alone of all the sacred books, the book of Esther never
mentions the name of God

vyehi biyemei Achashverosh

the story of Esther, who saves the Jews

Los Angeles

ladies and gentlemen: we are over
the coast of north America   flying
(see the green parrots in the palm trees?)
at an altitude of 10,700 meters
(see the possum among the vine leaves?)
an air speed of 927 km / h – and a bit more on the ground
(don't the figs look ripe?)
the temperature outside is -50° C
(good enough to eat)
another 2530 miles to go

SUNDAY

Main Street rubs its eyes; my feet find the sea's
                                        side
my legs work against the sand pull, a
marine magnet pulls me to Santa Monica pier
the day has no sense of time, and swimming
pools ignore the clouds

MONDAY

Chateau Camden and Little Jerusalem
rub grid shoulders here, where the man who sells
Yiddish and Klezmer still talks
out the fifties in rock and roll

Farmers' Market corned beef translates the salt
and luxury way back is everyone's
everyday here

the borscht belt is far away, in another jetlag

TUESDAY

in Hollywood the hills fold my star map
the Hispanic underclass in the heat
while their Sunset doesn't
                                        green grass must glow
among the tarmac   Hollywood lawns

a giant pair of billboard jeans threatens
to unzip my cool
the heat should not be romanticised
when a pavement telephone blinds the hand
that dials

in the cool of indoor *Chicago*, 'when
hell freezes over, I'll ski there'. She may
have done him wrong onstage
                                        but off, she skates
down the Avenue of the Stars

WEDNESDAY

Abbot's Habit tussles with longitude
and apple juice; in LA all abbots
have good habits

no-one can build a canal like
the Venetians who practised here before
imitating an earlier Venice
across another water

THURSDAY

Bessie Smith leans falling in another
Renaissance, a Harlem exhibition
jetlagged on her celluloid bar

FRIDAY

Rae's red plastic booths and a diner even
for a baby high chair
unseen men behind me discuss the
stock market: their stock should be cowboys, out
west clean shaven

sharing, not telling, says the good earth man
this is California

'I'm a Marxist and I believe in reading everything'
'That's a really Aries thing to say'

this is California

Mantegna and I
Andrea Mantegna, d. 13 September, 1506

in 1474, in between the Gonzaga figures
Mantegna has painted himself leaved in a
secret column
Andrea Mantegna watches Mantegna's face
watching

travelling reluctantly from Padua, Andrea, rubicund,
sneaks his mischievous brush into a distant blue and green
                                                    landscape
watched by horses and dogs, who snake fine white tails round
courtiers' red and white legs

a peacock pecks at the clouds above, in the oculus, the
ceiling's eye
ladies and Moors eavesdrop
putti poke each a watchful nakedness above the

plotting in the Camera Picta, the Camera degli Sposi, the
                                                    Camera Dipinta
where a painted room watches a married couple
whose marriage has been plotted by cardinals who look the
                                                    other way

these are men you can love
women you can smooth
solemn children who never learned to play

safe in his column, Mantegna's
sombre, tight face watches
fixed people sleeping easy on the walls, their eyes open

Andrea never sleeps
he watches in all our room
never trust an artist
expect nothing from art
except its watchfulness

owning up
for Julia

a wicker casket
with purple and green flowers
a suffragette, who
didn't need to be rescued
from the vote she'd won
to love us all forever

owning up to death
who owns death, who owns dying
did she own her death
                    don't ask her; she's gone

like the dawn I was before

it's called a freedom pass
not a passport to freedom
like the dawn I was before

not a border where you waited
with your suitcase
to stream through
with other refugees, other refusees
before dawn, like I was

then it was called the pension book
a proud freebie, reward for a life's work

now it's your turn; imagining it like the child benefit book
like the dawns they were
and when you go into the post office
you tuck
your grey hair behind the
newly permanent colour
red, like the dawn I never was
and the woman behind the counter
says, You're very modern
which I know I am or she wouldn't have
said

burning sage

sage brushes blue-grey leaves

once soft leaves, staining my hands moth-wing grey
now waiting, furled, rigid, waiting to flare
into nothing

a match lights and lights and lights, the London
damp folded into Arizona's blue-
grey furls

I tease out moisture to smoke protest, till
leaves dull the white bowl's shine with flame to flare
the blue-grey leaves

sage brush smoke rises upwards, in light-streaked
grey spirals, helix columns flaring and
winding to nothing

there is no wisdom or savour to bridge
dry and damp weather, the light and the dark
save sage

so I light and I light and I light, and
sage smiles flame into ash and the blue-grey
smokes into nothing

leaving me sage

snow and sewers in Berlin

I

Christmas brass in a café, street markets
Gluhwein warms church bells, Stollen as big as
a house

the passion of Kathe Kollwitz, her head
sunk over the head
                    of her dead
                              son
he craning backwards for the love
that never comes

snow falls above their heads through a circle
round for her head, round forever frozen
in the sky

during the day, the round sky is blue, the
sculpture black
                at night, no snow, the sky dark
mother and son glow golden

how can anyone live with the memory
of cruelty

II

guards frisk visitors to the New
Synagogue
                we place metal objects in
plastic boxes
                the difference is we

know we'll get these back
                         and gold doesn't count
as metal

beware small cruelties
                    they grow fast

    III

a café in snow in Berlin
                         apfel
strudel, thick custard. vanilla sauce and
whipped cream

a Swiss snow mountain, a skinny little
girl with large eyes, in a shiny kitchen
fed with slices of orange and thick whipped
cream

sitting high on a stool, spooning the whipped
white cream melting the orange round
                              snow whipped
white and she didn't have to finish the
dish

I used to recognise her

not really like Kathe Kollwitz, her head
sunk over the head
of her dead
son

he craning backwards for the love
that never comes

but still a child wanting a mother

    IV

the Brandenburg gate
                         a Russian trader
sells watches
                this belonged to an officer
I must find him and see if I can give
his life back

stones at

he shouted stones at
her cobbled heart
ashphalt roads designed with the rhythm
of failed architecture
                          a stone
sloughing off the stone that stalks my heart
pargeted patterns stuccoed in memory
swirls, an incised template

rue on her grave, no rosemary fragrance incensing her
                                              memory

the French lady at Christmas

I gave her my carrier bag,
the French lady
in the local café

careful eye shadow over pale eyes, smudged
down the edge of one cheek, where
shadow betrayed the mirror
a white trench coat, a dashing leopard scarf
trailing black velvet trousers
over cream espadrilles, in the chill December air

in the local café,
on the counter, buttered raisin cake shapes
are Christmas tree cutouts, pale cream butter
softening the currant shine

she explains she would like two to take home

a lemon yellow eggbox serves
quivers slightly in her black gloved hands,
on her way to the door

I offer her my carrier bag
thank you, she says
much easier to carry this way
thank you, and have a happy Christmas
by which I know

she will be alone,
like me

the Hidden God (or atheism)

the hidden god
came from Jerusalem
where else?

bubble-wrapped, with *rishon*, the first-class divine
                                        postage, odd
for a hidden god
who might want to stay
hidden

carefully uncellophaning the book
she feared her desire for genetic structuralism
                                        (*see hidden footnote*)
might shock all the gods
hidden
and revealed

but then, perhaps, expecting total loyalty
through doubt and pestilence

was a one-way street (*see hidden footnote for cultural refs*)
was wanting to have a cake and eat it (*see hidden footnote
                                        for cultural ref*)

and yet what else would you do with a cake
but eat it
and what would you do with a book, but read it, Good
                                        or Otherwise?

and why should a hidden god
be any different
from the rest of us

which is not to say that we are all gods
or perhaps it is
and we are (*see hidden footnote*)

dialectical haiku (intertextual)

1

which comes first? The li –
– terary text or the read –
– er? Which comes first? The

reader or the li –
– terary text? Which comes first?
the writer? Or the –

2

every teacher
is a teacher of English
because a teacher

in English   if
anyone   and
other, but

Samson after Milton

let there be light   light

guide me to
                light
where

I see   less

I am less   than   light

less
      eyeless
            no light

        let there be light

                  this is he
                  see, soft, how he lies
                  here he lies

                  once the strongest
                  now here he lies
                  once the envied of all

when I rest
do I choose
sun or shade   here he lies

when I wake
do I choose
sun or shade   once the strongest

the sun is dark now

silent the moon
deserts the night

      lie
      you lie
      you lied

      you betrayed
      you lost the light
      you lost the way
      now here you lie

my strength was given
and my strength was taken

my sin   to betray your friends

now my heart cannot see

noon's blaze does not warm me

the cool of dawn is forgotten

      remember

Silk Thistle or how the vote was won

Black Maria

tiny narrow cells
>> either side of a narrow gangway
>> ventilated by a grating in the floor
small holes on either side of the floor

wire netted ventilator
>> under the roof of the van
cupboards
>> knees tucked under my chin
>>>> cells filled
>> passage packed with prisoners
>>>> sardines
>>>>> can't stand upright

rumble jolting darkness bang jangle door

silence

it is the duty of the state to keep its prisoners alive
open your mouth and shut up

paper   scissors   stone

First date

>> violet blue eyes, clear olive skin, a warm flush
>> in your cheeks, jet black hair, fine-pencilled
>> eyebrows, a golden voice. A knot of scarlet
>> ribbon in my hair.

your hand opens the door of the cab.
I have arrived at the meeting.

brown velvet suitable for a wedding dress

POLITICS

a vote is green and purple with silver bars
a vote is a box with a cross in it
go into the box

cross your heart and be prepared to die

MEMORY

William Morris wallpaper and scarlet
lampshades
a dead boy in a bed
a sheet over his head

porridge and cod liver oil makes girls strong in the morning

I MEET A HERO

a narrow alley off Fetter Lane
dark winding stair
dark green woodwork
window seat
high, old-fashioned fireplace with hobs
engravings framed in polished rosewood
high narrow mantelpiece

                the hero cooks his own food
blacks his own boots
a miner
                            a collection of fossils
coal
bread, butter and Scotch scones
black coffee

he reads Shelley, Byron, William Morris

he remembers   daisies like the faces of little girls

                        pit ponies
in the dark

   PRISON I

I am charged with spitting in the face of a police officer
my arms are held
ten shillings
prison for seven days

fourteen days in the third division   prison dress
                                          prison cold porridge

votes for women
white calico
snatched away
white calico   white calico   white calico

dim stone corridors   filthy cells
high forbidding walls

40

                                    heavy doors
tall wardresses with jangling keys at their waists
pitch dark cubicles with a lidless WC

unfasten your chests
                                    undress
short coarse cotton chemise
hat, clothes and shoes on the shelf
                                    barefoot
raise your arms

    SILENCE

discoloured paint worn off the bath in patches
black iron, slimy and sodden
woodwork, slimy and sodden
water   scum

garments with a broad arrow
black on light colours   white on dark

harsh, thick woollen stockings   black
red rings round the legs
long red striped cotton drawers

                                                thick petticoat
bunched into a waistband
wide skirt   torn bodice

put on your stays
put on your shoes
stiff hard leather
                        laces which break as you tie them

                        41

white cap like a Dutch bonnet
strings under the chin
two pieces of cotton plaid, blue and white
one as an apron
one as a weekly handkerchief

no pockets   no garters

handkerchief hangs from the waistband by one corner
wide thick stockings flap around my ankles

six weeks without a change of clothing

PRISON II

                                                pavilions
tier upon tier of cells
doors studded with black nails
strong wire netting at each tier

                                        railings
a pair of sheets
a bible   a hymn book

'A Healthy Home and How to Keep It'
take a daily bath and sleep with open windows

CELL

seven feet by five
        stone floor
barred window

      flickering gas jet covered by a piece of tin
discoloured old wooden spoon
      wooden salt cellar
tin pint measure
      hard yellow soap
small scrubbing brush
      three-inch comb
mattress and blanket rolled up
      dust pan
water can
      wash basin
slop pail
      plank bed
thin towel wooden stool
      blankets and sheets too narrow

                no sleep

Day

before daylight, clatter, bells, feet

wash
      dress
empty slops
      roll up bedding
clean and polish tin with brick dust scoured up off the floor
      scrub floor, bed and table

thin gruel of oatmeal and water
      six ounces of brown bread
door slams

Protest I

seven thousand women in white
a giant bed of flowers
votes for women
self is forgotten
personality seems minute
the greatest meeting ever known

Arrest I

women rush in
                bruised
dishevelled
                     hatless
hair dragged down
                          false teeth knocked out
faces scratched
                                 eyes swollen
noses bleeding

a dog whip

Prison III

lights out   silence   doors   clang

airless   silence   echoes

tiny light   from high small windows
a stool   a shelfless table

                                    rolled-up bedding   plank bed
tins   wooden spoon   bible

thickish gruel   dark bread
                                      broth with floating
meat
               cocoa brew

solitary   chapel
                                              exercise

single file
high walled yard

                          silence

PROTEST II

climb scaffolding
                          lie concealed for hours
down through a skylight   hatchet to the chimney stacks
tear up slates   hurl them onto the roof of the hall
fire hose   take off shoes to avoid slipping
                                      on the wet slates
drenched clothes   blood streaming from wounds

ARREST II

police snatch flags   strike women with fists and knees
knock down kick drag carry fling black eyes bruises
                                              sprains

dislocations   wrists wrenched   thumbs   arms
                                       pinch arms
rub women's faces against the railings   pinch breasts
                                       squeeze ribs

BLACK FRIDAY

blaze of colour in the parks	scarlet caps
flaming red	purple, white and
green	
orange and green	black and white
green and gold	the red dragon
sombre black and brown	brilliant red and white
lilac robes	scarlet caps of liberty

PROTEST III

cushions in railways carriages slashed
flowerbeds damaged
old ladies apply for gun licences
gold greens burned with acid
votes for women burned with acid onto golfing
greens
telephone boxes severed with long handled clippers
envelopes containing red pepper and snuff sent to every
                                     cabinet minister
orchids torn up by the root at Kew Gardens
bombs in the bank of England

PRISON IV

five months for a window worth three pounds

hunger strike   thirst strike   hot and cold shivers
                                          pace the cell
crouch   kneel   pace   footsteps   wardresses
clutch a shoe   they close in on me   the shoe falls
fling me back on the bed   hold me by the shoulders
wrists   hips   ankles   doctors come   seize her by the
head   thrust a sheet under her chin   eyes shut   set
teeth   tighten lips   force open her mouth   I shall
suffocate   pull her lips apart   get inside   steel
instrument pressed on the gums

jerk my head   try and wrench it free   hold it   drag
                                          at her mouth
pant   heave   my breath   a low scream   a gap   steel
                          instrument cuts into gums

brace myself   stab of sharp, intolerable agony   I wrench
                                          my head free
they grasp   I struggle   a steel instrument cuts its
way in   my jaws forced apart   the screw is turned
they are trying to get the tube down my throat

                                vomit as the tube comes up
day after day
morning and evening

five steps to the window
                          turn
five steps back to the door

47

I shall not stop walking   walk till you come to feed me
then I shall walk again   throw myself against the wall
as I turn
my face is white   my eyes are like cups of
blood
my legs are sore and swollen   my joints are stiff
my pulse flutters like an insect's wing

                walk for twenty-eight hours

DREAM

tea and bread and butter
chops and steaks
jellies and fruit
water

nothing as sweet as the first draught of water after the
                        thirst strike

PRISON V

the sky through the bars is sombre grey, charged with yellow
        fire   from the light of London streets

blanket catches my foot   stumble   cold
cold   sky turns violet   sky dies to the bleak grey white
                        of early day
walk   walk again   legs ache   feet are
                    swollen and burning

                vote for me

dialectical: palimpsest / palindrome / barlines

I PALIMPSEST
a) NOUN

Paper parchment, etc., prepared for writing on and wiping out, like a slate.

history is a slate, continually written and rewritten, retaining traces behind each rewriting

not like a slate.

Is.

mossed   damp and greened

    scrape   a damp patch   patched dark in the sun

                    wiping spreads the wet

A paper, parchment, etc., on which the original writing has been effaced to make way for other writing; a manuscript in which a later writing is written over an effaced earlier writing.

the reputation of an author/composer is one thing during their lifetime; subsequently, their standing and cultural appropriation is continually

autobiography is far from   text

                    today I cried (*wept is too poetic*)

49

for a birthday

        the real me says nobody loves me and there is
nobody in the room to hear and the other real me

wonders about the next spaced   words

but and

                what real

                      what me

A monumental brass slab turned and re-engraved on
the reverse side.

*Claudio Monteverdi and Salamone Rossi: contemporary
composers and musicians in late 16th-early 17th century
Mantua*

        *Catholic and Jew
        musician at large and ghettoised citizen
        musical cusps
        Renaissance modes
        baroque treble/bass
        solo virtuoso*
        dramma per musica.

well

     but and   history   my history

my version of their history

        written to inform and pat into a new-old shape

damp round its edges

         let us not forget

they are dead

      and I am not

              yet

but and

              engrave my lines

b) Adjective

Of a manuscript: having the original writing effaced and
superseded by later writing.

*fiction and music are composed via a process of writing and
rewriting, of rewriting and writing*

              re

reading   comes before and after

  during

let us and me be very clear

                         writing is not reading
                                 and reading not writing is

but

        missing   intertextuality, a word

I may never want to hear

                                                 and but

Of a monumental brass: turned and re-engraved on
the reverse.

*music and words use different notational systems. The term
'language' is applied to written systems, which (pace Saussure
et al) consist of arbitrary signs combined into notational forms,
which we use in verbal and written ways to communicate,
to create and transmit meanings read by us, and to compose
artefacts, artworks, which we call fiction. In music the systems
loosely resemble some of the features of mathematics, resonant
with patterns and meanings, the heuristic analysis of which
in musicology lags far behind work on verbal language. The
issue of 'meaning' in and around music is vexed, contested,
muddled and linked with the significance of words in music
— sung sound*

Word or phrase that reads the same backwards as forwards.

Western music reads from left to right, Hebrew from right to left. Salamone Rossi rsn the two systems: the music 'reads' from left to right, the Hebrew words are placed below the notes in their readable

right

to

left

form.

right   and   left

mirrors in space

once upon a time there was a story, which started at the beginning and started at the end, meeting itself in the middle

up

and

down

down   up

once upon a time there was a choirbook so big that everyone could stand round it each reading their music from their own page. The music faced north, south, east and west. This is called a table layout

the words   north   east   south and

       west

are arbitrary

    they could just as easily be a table set on a globe

         that is not the case with me

I am here

    and now

        now you may see me, or think me

and now everyone on the other arbitrary side

          doesn't

Music: Piece in which the second half is a retrograde
repetition of the first half.

*experimentation with the influence of form on content and
content on form will*

read backwards and forwards
        sdrawrof dna sdrawkcab daer

         draw   dna   draw

Vertical line drawn through the musical stave to mark off metrical units.

Polyphonic vocal music of the Renaissance was not notated in bars. In England, barlines of irregular length are found in keyboard sources as late as the Fitzwilliam Virginal Book, written after 1621.

what are the boundaries of knowledge? What happens to existing structures of knowledge when new information is uncovered?

the sound of music from the inside   is silence

illuminatus

1

in the city of London
there is a book
made from mulberries and willow
where the duties of the heart are gilded
into devotion

                        golden words chase across the sky

someone said, let there be light
and the book was illuminated

a book is a house where
words live
sounding like birds

2

a book carries the
fingerprints of alchemy
hand-coloured, each finger
another hue

a book is a house
and through it runs
the river of Paradise
                        in the city of London, there is a book

3

       in the city of York, there is a story

in the city of York
cold stone cries
fire bleeds
paper smoulders

here the knife cuts
here stones fall

stone   paper   knife

       in the city of York there is a story

4

in the year one thousand one hundred and eighty nine
Richard, the son of Henry the Second,
came to the throne of England

        did it rain
        did the sun shine
        did the leaves fall
        in rain or sun

5

in the city of York
many people take an oath against the Jews

the Jews entreat the governor of the royal castle for mercy
the Jews retreat to the castle for safety

> did it rain or did it shine
> did the leaves fall
> in sun or rain

6

bands of armed men from city and country
surround the castle
stone walls crumble like charred paper

an elder speaks
we must prefer
a glorious death to an infamous life
an honourable and easy death

> did it rain or did it shine
> does the sun have eyes
> does the rain tell the story

7

the roof of the castle is set on fire

look how we can dance in the flames

the sun on the stone
the stone beneath the sun

                              the castle is filled with a cloud

8

        In the year 1290, all estates belonging to the Jews
are seized, and the entire community is banished from
the realm

                        in the beginning was the expulsion

the saints watch the first country of Christendom
whence the Jews are expelled, without hope of return

now, by the ground that we are banished from
we could curse away a winter's night
England is the first country of Christendom whence
                              the Jews are banished

                the we are estranged from ourselves

        Ora pro nobis

9

we embrace and kiss and take ten thousand leaves
we find an age of discord and continual strife
a time when words are no longer music to our ears
when objects are not pleasing in our eyes
when touch is not welcome to our hands

to see, to hear, to touch
these are no longer in perfect sympathy

        we are estranged from ourselves
lacking even a glass
wherein to see our shadows as we pass

10

    in the year 1492, Ferdinand, called the Catholick,
being King of Spain, drove out of his country all
the Jews that were living there from the time of the
Babylonian and Roman captivity

in the year 1497, at the request of the said King
Ferdinand, the Jews were banished out of Portugal

        the Jews are banished from England,
                Spain and Portugal

11

     in Queen Elizabeth's England there is a story

Queen Elizabeth's England is gilded with strawberries in
red wine
sugar, cinnamon and ginger
mace and saffron
rose water
and cloth of gold

     in Queen Elizabeth's England, there is a secret story

beware the secret taste of sharp, fresh ginger in the mouth

12

in the city of London
the larks make sweet division
soft stillness and the night
become the touches of sweet harmony
while families close their doors
light their candles
and speak in other tongues
subtle as the sphinx

13

    in early seventeenth-century London there are over 10,000 aliens
French, Dutch, Spaniards, Portuguese, a small number of black people

and Jews

                Marranos
                New Christians. Converts. New converts.
                New Christians. Conversos.

a Marrano is one descended from Jews or infidels, whose parents were never christened, but for to save their goods, will say that they are Christians.

a Marrano is a Jew counterfeitly turned Christian

how can you recognise a false Jew
 a secret Jew
a counterfeit Christian
how can you really tell the difference between a Christian
                              and a Jew

                    what's in a name

New Christians must be secret Jews if they do not eat pork
if they use olive oil rather than lard
when they change their bed linen every Friday
when they call their children by Old Testament names
when they pray in a strange tongue, standing rather than
                                                    kneeling
when they turn to face a wall, on hearing of a death

in Queen Elizabeth's England
families close their doors
light their candles
and speak in other tongues
subtle as the sphinx

    14

Elizabeth is of fair complexion
marigolds are good to dye hair fair
what is the right name for a colour

hair can be coloured black with elderberries or yellow
with marigolds
what's in a colour
                              what's in a name

15

in the City of London
pleasure gardens grow

nasturtiums from Peru, Mexican marigolds, lilies and
                                                    sweet potatoes
tomatos and mulberries
peaches and apricots, roses and clematis, larkspur and delphinium
yellow foxgloves, lilac and laburnum

out of every hundred babies born alive in the City of London
in the seventeenth century
some may have been Jewish

                                        what's in a name

16

                                        what's in a name
a name is secret as a sphinx in the night
a word unlike
other words

you can as soon kindle fire with snow
as quench the fire of love with other words

in between times of night and day
false and real words are as shadows in a glass
even a summer's day turns dark when the sun passes

                            imagine a rose without a name

17

one name becomes two names
one story becomes two stories

        this is the story of two peoples
        this is the story of two people

Menasseh ben Israel
and Oliver Cromwell

18

in Amsterdam, a man called Menasseh ben Israel
drinks tea
by a canal
in Holland's green and pleasant land

in Huntingdon, in England's green and pleasant land
a man called Oliver Cromwell brews beer
a gentleman, living neither in considerable height
nor yet in obscurity
amid lush green meadows, watery and windswept

        this is the story of dreams
of promised lands
and broken promises
of prophecies and of the music of dreams

19

Menasseh and Oliver share a dream
seen from pleasant lands shrouded in fog

                the dust of dreams is carried on the
      wind

20

a learned, distinguished Jew, born in Lisbon and
                              resident in Holland
turns his eyes to England

England is the centre of the universe
destined to pave the way for the Messiah

Oliver looks to the Jews
destined to help pave the way for the Second Coming

the Jews will bring with them trade into England
cinnamon and cardamom, nutmeg, mace and black
pepper
pomegranates, emeralds
and cloves
silk, cotton and mohair
raisins, dates, dried figs and coffee
Persian silk, phosphorus, white pepper

and ginger, tamed to the root

21

this is the story of two people
this is the story of two peoples

the story of two men

Menasseh ben Israel and Oliver Cromwell
sit in the coffee house
as ordinary as
a merchant banker
an insurance underwriter
a broker
a musician
a journalist

two people drink from small coffee cups
delicate bone china
thick black Turkish coffee
from the Levant via Venice

a bitter black drink
boiled with egg shells
mixed with mustard, oatmeal, ginger or butter
to help digestion, quicken the spirits
good against coughs and consumption, dropsy, gout and scurvy

coffee is the alchemy which turns life into gold and treasure
coffee tastes like home

22

Oliver and Menasseh
meet in the coffee house
at banquets and at masques
speaking in the shared tongues of poetry

had we but world enough and time
this leisure, Cromwell, were no crime
we would sit down, drink our coffee
and pass our friendship's day

thou, by the Thames' side
should'st rubies find: I, by Holland's tide
should speak and write

I should be your friend forever, and forever refuse
to countenance the Conversion of the Jews

the sun itself which makes times, as they pass
is elder by some time, now, than it was
when thou and I first one another saw
all other things, to their destruction draw,
only our friendship has no decay

theologians may explain the world
our job is to change it

        let us not to the marriage of our true minds
        admit impediments

23

a special conference is set up
a notable gathering of sixteen theologians and divines
lawyers, justices and merchants
to consider whether it be lawful to receive the Jews
into England's green and pleasant land

all the arguments are put
all the fears rehearsed

if the Jews are admitted
they will buy St Paul's Cathedral and the Bodleian Library
admission of the Hebrews will enrich foreigners and
                                        impoverish the natives

24

after the conference
after the theologians and divines have debated
after the lawyers, justices and merchants have argued
answers are given

                    a definite legal opinion is given

there is no law which forbids the return of the Jews to England

so Jews have been secretly legal all the time
ever since 1290

and yet
nothing is formally concluded touching the point of
their admission

                                  there is nothing formal
nothing official
no report formally accepted
no action officially taken
no formal order of readmission is made

25

while Oliver Cromwell lives near
the vines that flourish in Leicester fields
the peonies and the gooseberries
the mulberries and the figs and the morello cherries

while all these grow
there is
informal
permission to worship, as long as it is in private houses

there is
informal
permission for
a house to be rented as a synagogue
in Cree Church Lane
for
a plot of land to be bought
in a cemetery
in Mile End

the ground has been secretly opened
with stone, paper and knife

26

in the city of London
a book made from mulberries and willow
paints golden words against the sky

a book is a house where
words live
sounding like birds

                        a book is a house
                        and through it runs
                        the river of Paradise

◊PHELIA

*p*rays, *h*emmed, *e*ncastled, *l*onely, *i*ntimating
*a*nother

   motherless, perhaps betrayed

   1

Ophelia lies on
the river bank
watching stars in the
water; shielding her hair's shine

                          the sky

streams tears
a curtain to the ground

                    I am Narcissus, thinks Ophelia

still as stone
fluid as moon opal in the sun
my own Echo

black is the colour of gravity
the moon a moist star
                    I am opal

                          melting

2

water is its

        its own

               its own music

changing scales at will
rushing chords with wind and rain
singing monody in lazy summer lines
when sky and stream dip divisions
in every ripple

          a soundless night

has no water to hear it

there is no definite article
everything is indefinite

        in forever water

3

Ophelia melts into
water silking along her sides
no salt to dull her

over her back
one like flows into another like
skinwet, shining round-soft
apple-hungry

seeing under the water is believing
in the water

4

the water mirror

looks into the depths of the earth
where glacier vapours glow red

        pinnacles of a crystal palace

tip red glass-glaciers and red ice spires

vespers
   whisper wafers and holy water

5

Ophelia mirrors the past tense
                    in her room, books around her

she walks widdershins
a willow woman
a little more than kin and less than kind

in one book she is a boy
with an as-yet no beard

in one she sees her Hamlet, sweet, not lasting
his vows slimy under water
                    a frog   if not kissed

in another, she is warned to read no letters
to drown her love
to listen to a jealous brother
an overprotective father
a might-have-been mother in law

Ophelia peers into her

                                        mirror
cannot see her

                                        mother

6

          in her mirror Ophelia languishes, aches
prays   aches
reads   aches

at night she walks by the river
sometimes blue, sometimes green
sometimes colours moving so
fast, they do not wait for
                              names

          Ophelia stands on a glass bridge
her naked feet
upside-down   to   a   water self
opal pads flex chill toes

          the water will love me

7

Ophelia smashes water glass

                                          rose

filaments hairing lines in the

                                          water

Ophelia humours her humour
considers madness, breaks the

                                        strings

on her lute and

                          laughs

lets her hair down and

                            laughs

being honest and fair are not the same

                                          she sings

unless I make them

                                                          so

8

Ophelia melts through the water
twines her helix legs

a mermaid
a devil with a fish's tail
a devil in the water

                              shape-shifter

sings bubbles to sweeten tempted ships

strings her harp, to find magic between the

                              strings

those who have not seen a mermaid
those who have seen a mermai
those who have seen a merma
those who have seen a merm
those who have seen a mer
those who have seen a me
those who have seen a m
those who have not seen a

                              disappear

                                    have not seen

9

a feather, a wing

a duckling, grey, the last grey of the grey
litter, last in the water, last on the land
bobbing on the water, between
fin and hair and scales and skin

where the duckling touches her, Ophelia is
feathered, opalescent in the morning sun

six swans land in a circle, blow each others' feathers
stand, shivering, in their six soft skins
blow their six skins into six silk cloaks

six princes stand tall and beautiful

the duckling smiles
Ophelia smiles

10

Ophelia imagines a
prince
with skin
        soft as swansdown
eyes
        flashing
                fireweed like kingfisher
                                flowers
                                waterweed
reminds her to shed her skin

11

I shed my skin against fennel

                                      sweet and wild

drink fennel juice

                                        stroke fronds

against my new skin

            I will boil my heart with fennel to make

                                            my love

digestible

my stems will be soft and tender and white
my leaves will steep in barley water
and I will cause good habits in my body

12

I am rosemary, sweet, dark and green

                              smell me

here and here and here

I will remember you, be with you at

                              your wedding
                              your burying

I will blow away evil dreams
if you are unfaithful I will

                    prick

your skin and you will

                    bleed

                              sap

13

I am columbine, an eagle
my talons flower pink and purple
I land on you like a flight of doves
and carry you
                to heartsease   because

wild thoughts, pansy lick-leaves
your love in idleness
will lie bleeding
                                because
instead of putting your foot on seven daisies to find
                        when summer has come
you have trodden on glass
                        and you
                        will rue
                        the day you made me
a sour herb of grace

                        bitter
                        keep away

14

the moon falls upwards
                        back
into the sky
gravity turns from   black
to midnight to opal dawn sheen

        Ophelia resolves into a dew, untwines her helix
tail and falls upwards   back
onto the   bank
armpits flavoured with fennel and rosemary and
remembrance
pansies in her thoughts

        Ophelia strokes her swan feathers into silk
breathes the breath of alchemy's quintessence

water reminds her of her groundling love

there can never be too much of water
no fire
        can put this water out

Biographical Note

MICHELENE WANDOR is a playwright, poet, fiction writer and musician. She is the first woman playwright to have had a drama on one of the National Theatre's main stages – *The Wandering Jew*, in 1987, the same year her adaptation of *The Belle of Amherst* won an International Emmy for Thames TV. Her prolific radio drama includes original radio plays and dramatisations (novels by Dostoyevsky, Jane Austen, George Eliot, Kipling, Sara Paretsky and Margaret Drabble), many nominated for awards. Her books on contemporary theatre include *Postwar British Drama: Looking Back in Gender*.

In 2002 she received a Millennium Lottery Fund Award, to make a CD of the music of Salamone Rossi, early seventeenth-century Jewish Mantuan composer.

Her poetry collection, *Gardens of Eden Revisited*, and her book of short stories, *False Relations*, are published by Five Leaves. Her book about the history and practice of creative writing in the UK, *The Author is Not Dead, Merely Somewhere Else*, was published by Palgrave Macmillan in 2008. She has held a Royal Literary Fund Fellowship since 2004.

Her previous two poetry collections, *Musica Transalpina* and *The Music of the Prophets*, were published by Arc; the former was a Poetry Book Society Recommendation for Spring 2006.

Selected titles in Arc Publications'
POETRY FROM THE UK / IRELAND include: